BACK-TO-SCHOOL
PROJECTS
FOR A
LAZY
CRAFTERNOON

BY STELLA FIELDS

CAPSTONE PRESS
a capstone imprint

Lazy Crafternoon and Snap are published by
Capstone Press
A Capstone imprint
1710 Roe Crest Drive
North Mankato, Minnesota 56003
www.mycapstone.com

Library of Congress Cataloging-in-Publication Data is available on the
Library of Congress website.

ISBN: 978-1-5157-1438-5

Summary: Use this craft book to spend a lazy crafternoon making
school supply projects with your friends.

Designer: Lori Bye
Creative Director: Heather Kindseth
Photos: Karon Dubke/Capstone Studio

Projects crafted by Lori Blackwell, Mari Bolte, Lori Bye,
Sarah Holden, Heather Kindseth, Marcy Morin, Sarah Schuette

Image credits: Shutterstock: Ann Haritonenko, 5 (top right), Jenn Huls, 25, nenetus, 5 (top left),
Pressmaster, back cover, 5 (bottom)

Design Elements: Shutterstock: ARaspopova, luanateutzi, pixelliebe, Studio Lulu, Tossaporn Sakkabanchom

Special thanks to Dede Barton, Shelly Lyons, and Mari Bolte

Printed and bound in the USA.
009687F16

CONTENTS

LAZY CRAFTERNOON

A lazy crafternoon is a day you spend with your friends, each of you making something incredible. Doesn't sound lazy, right? But it can feel like it, especially with the fun, pretty projects in this book.

These projects can be done on your own — nothing requires more than one person — but it's always more fun to spend a lazy crafternoon making things with your friends. The crafts in this book are great for beginners, but they can be taken to a new level by crafters with more experience. Invite girls who already craft on their own, but don't stop there. Your fashionista friend already has a great sense for fabric. Your musician friend knows how to put things together. Your movie-loving friend has an eye for what looks great.

You'll need plenty of supplies. You can choose projects from this book and stock the supplies yourself, or just ask your friends to bring what they have. Many of the projects here use things you already have around the house.

Before your friends arrive, get everything set up in your crafting space. You can craft on your bedroom floor or outside, but you might want to find a table where you can lay out the supplies and have room for everyone to work.

Don't forget snacks! Treats on sticks or cut into small, bite-sized pieces are great choices for people who don't want to get their hands dirty mid-craft. Check out page 28 for a perfect drink to serve your friends (and a craft to go along with it), and page 30 for a snack that's just right for crafting.

That's it! Now get lazy.

SUPPLIES

alphabet stickers
box
button
colored yarn
cotton webbing
decoupage glue
elastic ribbon
fabric
fabric glue
glass bottle
hot glue

paper clips
paintbrush
paper punch
pencil
pins
ribbon
rubbing alcohol
scissors
scrapbook paper

hot glue gun
inspirational stickers
iron
keyboard
laptop computer
large photo frame
magazines
needle and thread
notebook
oil-based markers

sewing machine
sheet of foam
spray paint
thumbtacks
twine
washi tape
wax paper
white glue
white mugs

FANCY PENCILS

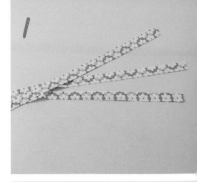

WHAT YOU'LL NEED

fabric
scissors
twine
pencils
white glue
hot glue or small headpins

1. Cut fabric into strips that are about 24 inches (60 cm) long and 0.5 inch (1.2 cm) wide.

2. Fold a strip in half, and then keep folding until the strip is about 3 inches (7.5 cm) long.

3. Use the twine to tie the fabric in the middle. Then cut the folded ends.

4. Fluff up the fabric to make a pom-pom.

5. Cover a pencil in white glue. Wrap a piece of fabric around and down the length of the pencil.

6. Use hot glue or small headpins to attach the pom-pom to the ends of the pencil.

Before you sharpen these pencils, pull the fabric away and cut off the amount you'll sharpen.

9

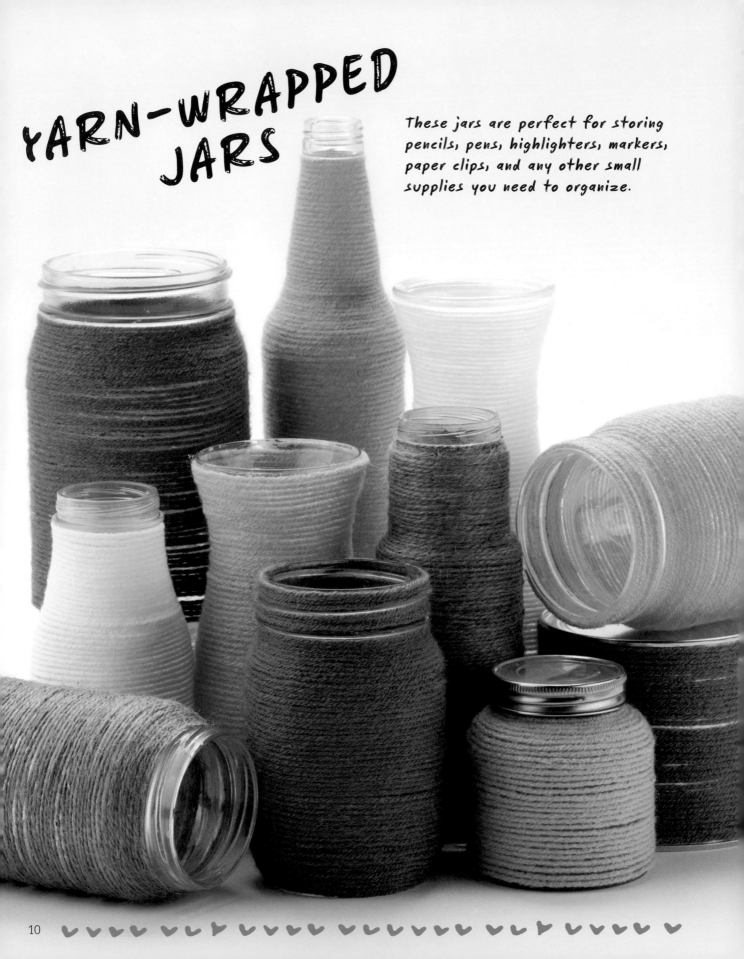

YARN-WRAPPED JARS

These jars are perfect for storing pencils, pens, highlighters, markers, paper clips, and any other small supplies you need to organize.

WHAT YOU'LL NEED

hot glue and hot glue gun
glass bottle
colored yarn
scissors
white glue

1 Use hot glue to attach a yarn strand near the top of
   the bottle.

2 Starting at the top of the jar or bottle, cover a section
   with white glue, and then wrap the yarn over the
   glued portion. Make sure the loops of yarn are tight
   and as close together as possible. Continue wrapping
   and gluing.

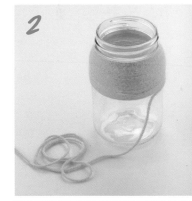

3 If you want to change colors, just snip the yarn and
   secure the loose end with more hot glue. Then continue
   wrapping and gluing with a new color of yarn.

4 When you reach the bottom of the jar, cut the yarn and
   use hot glue to seal the end.

You can yarn-wrap more than just bottles! Wooden
letters, flower pots, wreaths, and even furniture
(think chair legs) are all easy to wrap.

Why should homework be boring?

WASHI TAPE SCHOOL SUPPLIES

PAPER CLIPS

/ Simply loop washi tape around paper clip and trim the edge.

WHAT YOU'LL NEED

paper clips
pencils
scissors
washi tape
wax paper
paper punch
notebook

PENCILS

1 Cut a strip of washi tape that is the same length as a pencil.

2 Stick the cut strip onto the pencil and carefully wrap it, making sure there are no air bubbles.

3 Repeat with a second strip to completely cover.

These are quick to make, so make extras—your friends will want their own.

NOTEBOOK STICKERS

1 Place a strip of washi tape on wax paper.

2 Use a paper punch to cut the sticker design out of the washi tape and wax paper.

3 Peel the washi tape sticker off of the wax paper backing and place it onto a notebook.

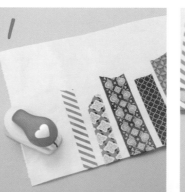

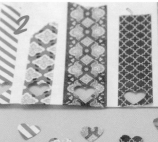

Decorate your desk with these pretty paperweights.

PAINTED ROCKS

1 Clean your rocks with warm water and let dry.

2 Choose your pattern or art and begin painting. You can use paint to cover the rock completely, or use painting pens for small details, or both!

3 Once your painted rock is dry, apply a layer of clear decoupage glue or protective lacquer. Let it dry and add one more layer.

Try writing short phrases or words on your rocks for little uplifters.

COLORFUL COMPUTER

You're not a plain Jane, and your computer doesn't have to be either.

WHAT YOU'LL NEED

washi tape
scissors
keyboard
laptop computer

1. For the keyboard: cut washi tape to fit the keys.

2. For the laptop: Cut 13 strips of washi tape, each about 15 inches (38 cm) long. Lay seven of them down on your laptop lid, diagonally from top left to bottom right. Don't stick them down hard—just place them there.

3. Place one strip so that it is perpendicular to the strips you've already put down. Working one strip at a time, weave it over and under the other strips. Continue with the other five strips.

4. Trim the edges of the tape.

Leave some keys uncovered—or use clear washi tape—for maximum effect (and so you know where your fingers are supposed to go).

RIBBON ORGANIZER

Assignments, photos, notes, memorabilia—save it all in this pretty organizer.

WHAT YOU'LL NEED

18 x 22 inch (45 x 56 cm) photo frame

spray paint

thumbtacks

fabric (2 inches (5 cm) larger on each side than the photo frame)

hot glue gun and hot glue

scissors

9-foot- (3-m-) long piece of ½-inch- (1.2-cm-) wide ribbon

4

5

6

8

1. Take the photo frame apart. Set the cardboard backing aside, and discard the glass.

2. Set the frame on a protected work surface in a well-ventilated area. Color the frame with spray paint. Let the paint dry and repeat with a second coat, if desired. Set aside.

3. Spray paint the thumbtacks.

4. Lay the fabric pattern-side-down. Lay the cardboard over the fabric. Wrap the edges of the fabric tightly around the back of the cardboard. Hot glue the fabric edges to the back of the cardboard.

5. Cut the ribbon into two 26-inch (66-cm) strips and three 20-inch (50-cm) strips. Arrange the strips in a crisscross pattern on the front of the board.

6. Use thumbtacks to hold the ribbons in place where they cross.

7. Turn the board over. Pull the end of one ribbon tight to the back of the board and hot glue in place. Repeat with both ends of all ribbons.

8. Reassemble photo frame.

PERSONALIZED NOTEBOOKS

Whether you're taking notes in class or keeping a journal, you'll love having these bright books to work in.

DECOUPAGE

1. Paint a thin layer of decoupage glue on the front cover of the notebook.

2. Place scrapbook paper over notebook cover. Press down firmly to remove any unwanted air bubbles.

3. Flip notebook to inside front cover and fold over excess scrapbook paper on each side. Cut several slits in each corner to allow folds to contour around the corners if rounded.

4. Apply decoupage glue to folded-over paper and corners.

5. Flip notebook over and repeat steps 1-4 on the back cover.

6. Wrap the spine of your notebook with several strips of washi tape, starting in the middle and working toward the top and bottom of the notebook. Wrap the extra tape onto the inside, and trim to fit.

7. Decorate with inspirational stickers, letters, pictures, cut-outs from magazines, etc. using decoupage glue.

WHAT YOU'LL NEED

notebook
decoupage glue
paintbrush
scrapbook paper
alphabet stickers
inspirational stickers
magazines
washi tape
scissors

WASHI

1. Wrap the notebook horizontally with strips of washi tape.

2. Wrap the notebook's spine vertically.

3. Trim the edges of the washi tape.

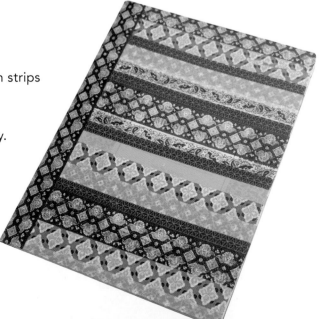

QUICK FABRIC TOTE

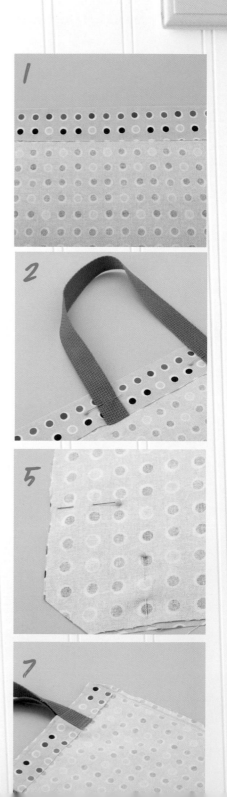

1. Lay one piece of fabric pattern-side-down. Fold the top edge in 1.5 inches (4 cm). Iron the fold.

2. Pin both ends of one webbing handle onto the fold.

3. Sew along the top and bottom of the fold. Make sure to sew the handles down as well.

4. Repeat steps 1-3 with the second pieces of fabric and webbing.

5. Pin the bag halves together, patterned sides in. Snip the bottom corners off; this will help the bag look more finished.

6. Sew 0.5 inch (1.2 cm) from the edges to join the halves together. Use a backstitch when you get to each end of the seam.

7. Use a zigzag stitch along the very edges of the bag. This will prevent the fabric edges from fraying.

8. Turn the bag right side out. It's ready to use!

Carry your books in style!

DIY TABLET COVER

WHAT YOU'LL NEED

sheet of foam

0.5 yard (0.5 m) of fabric

iron

0.25-inch- (0.6-cm) wide elastic ribbon

button

needle and thread (or sewing machine)

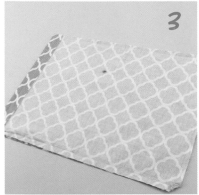

1. Trace and cut out your tablet's shape onto the foam. Repeat for a second piece.

2. Set the foam shapes onto the fabric. Leave 0.5 inch (1.2 cm) between the pieces of foam. Trace 0.5 inch (1.2 cm) around the outside of the foam. Allow 1 inch (2.5 cm) of fabric on the left side of the foam. Cut out the fabric piece. Repeat to make a second piece.

3. Fold the left edges of the fabric pieces in 0.5 inch (1.2 cm), and iron in place.

4. Place the fabric pieces on top of each other, wrong sides out. Sew along the top, bottom, and right sides of the fabric, leaving 0.25 inch (0.6 cm) for a seam allowance.

5. Trim the corners of the seams for a clean fold. Then turn the cover inside out, so the bright sides of the fabric are out.

6. Slip the foam pieces into the fabric case. Leave 0.5 inch (1.2 cm) between the pieces.

7. Pin the left edges of the fabric together, and sew closed. Sew three lines of stitches up the center of the cover to create a spine.

8. Set the tablet on the right side of the cover. Pin elastic in all four corners. When it's placed how you want, sew the elastic in place.

9. Sew a button to the front of the cover. Sew a loop of elastic to the back of the cover, to keep the cover closed.

You can make this for any brand of tablet. It's way more fun than going to a store and buying a boring, plain cover.

Don't just hide your special stuff in shoeboxes. These pretty fabric boxes bring a splash of color.

FABRIC-COVERED BOXES

WHAT YOU'LL NEED

fabric
pencil
scissors
box with a bottom and a lid
fabric glue

1. Place the fabric pattern side down on your work surface. Set the box in the center of the fabric and trace around the edges. Don't cut on this line — you'll need it later.

2. Measure and cut the fabric to the height of the box, plus 1 inch (2.5 cm). You'll wrap the entire box, so make sure the fabric is wide enough to stretch from the top of one side along the bottom and to the top of the other side.

3. Pick up the box and apply fabric glue to the bottom. Set the box back onto the fabric, making sure it sits inside the lines you drew in step 1.

4. Make a cut from the corner of the fabric square to the nearest box corner. Repeat with all four corners.

5. Fold one long side of the fabric up and tuck it inside the box. Use fabric glue to hold it in place. Repeat with the other long side of the fabric.

6. Repeat step 5 with the short sides of the box.

7. Repeat steps 1-5 with the box's lid.

Two presents in one! Use one of these boxes as a perfect way to give a gift. No wrapping paper to throw away, and your giftee can use it for storage of her own.

27

A delicious treat in her own personalized mug? Perfect. Make these ahead of time for a sweet surprise.

HAND-PAINTED MUGS & PINK VELVET HOT CHOCOLATE

WHAT YOU'LL NEED

For the mugs:
white mugs
rubbing alcohol
oil-based markers

For the hot chocolate:
2 tablespoons (30 grams)
    unsweetened cocoa
1 tablespoon (15 grams)
    chocolate chips
2 tablespoons (30 grams) sugar
¼ cup (59 ml) water
2 cups (500 ml) milk
¼ teaspoon (1 ml) vanilla
pink food coloring

Try personalizing each mug with a friend's name, or using the same few colors so that each mug coordinates with the others.

The design on these mugs will stand up to hand washing, but it may start to come off in the dishwasher.

MUGS

1 Wipe down the mug with rubbing alcohol.

2 Draw your design on your mug.

3 Place your mug(s) on a cookie sheet and place in a cold oven.

4 Allow to preheat to 350 degrees F (180 degrees C) and bake for a total of thirty minutes.

5 Cool in the oven, and make sure you let the mugs cool thoroughly before touching them— they'll be hot for a few hours. Wash your mugs before using for Pink Velvet Hot Chocolate.

HOT CHOCOLATE

1 Combine cocoa, chocolate chips, sugar, and water in a mug. Microwave for 30 seconds, then stir. Microwave for another 30 seconds, or until the chocolate chips are completely melted. Stir everything well.

2 Slowly add milk and vanilla. Stir, and heat for one to two minutes, or until hot. Stir in food coloring.

SWEET SNACK

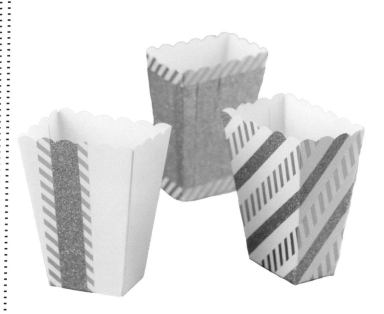

WHAT YOU'LL NEED

5 cups (about 85 grams) popped
   popcorn

1 cup (about 100 grams) pretzels

¼ cup (about 25 grams) mini
   marshmallows

¼ cup (about 25 grams) each of pink
   candy melts, chocolate candies, pastel
   sprinkles, and purple candy melts

½ cup (about 50 grams) pastel
   chocolate candies

1   Spread popcorn, pretzels, and marshmallows onto a baking sheet lined with parchment paper.

2   Place one color candy melts in a sandwich bag. Melt in a microwave at 50% power for one minute. Squeeze bag to stir candy melts. Melt for another 30 seconds or until candy is completely melted.

3   Snip the end off the sandwich bag and drizzle candy melts over the popcorn and marshmallows.

4   Sprinkle a third of the chocolate candies and sprinkles over the drizzled candy melts.

5   Repeat steps 2-4 with the other candy melts.

6   Place the baking sheet in a freezer for five minutes or until chocolate is hardened.

Cover popcorn boxes—available at grocery and craft stores—with glittery washi tape in different patterns.

You can fill these boxes with any munchable you and your friends love!

31

READ MORE

Bolte, Mari. *Eco Gifts: Upcycled Gifts You Can Make.* Make It, Gift It. North Mankato, Minn.: Capstone Press, 2016.

Kadichurian, Debbie. *Bring on the Bling!.* Accessorize Yourself. North Mankato, Minn.: Capstone Press, 2016.

Laz, Ashley Ann. *Totally Washi!: More Than 45 Super Cute Washi Tape Crafts for Kids.* Avon, Mass.: Adams Media, 2014.

INTERNET SITES

FactHound offers a safe, fun way to find Internet sites related to this book. All of the sites on FactHound have been researched by our staff.

Here's all you do:
Visit www.facthound.com
Type in this code: 9781515714385

LOOK FOR ALL THE BOOKS IN THE SERIES